THE ABORTION AGENDA
Considering the Irish Context

THE TRAGIC TOLL OF ABORTION
What are the effects on the Mother, the Unborn Baby, the Doctor, and Society?

Kieran Beville

THE ABORTION AGENDA

Considering the Irish Context

Kieran Beville

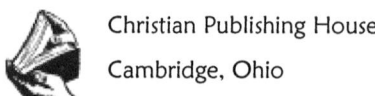

Christian Publishing House
Cambridge, Ohio

Copyright © 2016 Kieran Beville

All rights reserved. Except for brief quotations in articles, other publications, book reviews, and blogs, no part of this book may be reproduced in any manner without prior written permission from the publishers. For information, write, support@christianpublishers.org

Unless otherwise indicated, Scripture quotations are from the Updated American Standard Version of the Holy Scriptures, 2016 edition (UASV).

THE ABORTION AGENDA: Considering the Irish Context

Authored by Kieran Beville

ISBN-13: **978-1-945757-23-5**

ISBN-10: **1-945757-23-X**

Table of Contents

Foreword 1
When Does Human Life Begin? 2
Baby in a Bucket 4
Stop the Torture and Killing of Unborn Children Coming to Ireland. 5
Should the 8th Amendment be Repealed? 7
    Intense Focus 7
    Lessons from Other Countries 7
    Principle and Pragmatism 7
    Political Moves 7
    Pro-choice Rallies 8
    Being Visible and Vocal 8
    Repeal the 8th? 9
Abortion Coming to Ireland? 10
    Restrictions 10
    Citizen's Assembly 10
    What Next? 10
    Opinion and Expectations 11
    Mood Music 11
Abortion: Unmasking the Liberal Agenda in Ireland 12
    Callous and Cruel 12
    UNHRC Rebuke 13
    Being Lectured 13
    Time for Change 14
Amnesty International want Permissive Abortion in Ireland 16
Blackadder ~ Ireland's Minister for Children and Abortion 20
"Amnesty International" or "Damn Nasty International" 22
"A World Without Down's Syndrome" ~ A Review 26
Abortion in Cases of Rape 30
Abortion in cases of foetal abnormalities 32
Abortion ~ think about it 33

The Neoliberal Bandwagon is in Town 38
The Bridge between Abortion and Euthanasia Is Infanticide 41
    Times have Changed 43

Foreword

The Abortion Agenda: Considering the Irish Context ~ The Eighth Amendment of the Constitution of Ireland introduced a ban on abortion by recognising the right to life of an unborn child. This is now under scrutiny, and a campaign is underway to "Repeal the $8^{th.}$" This well-organised crusade is heavily funded by foreign money, and there is pressure being brought to bear on Ireland by international bodies, like the United Nations and Amnesty International. It is important, therefore, that people are informed. Although this book is intended to address the Irish context at a specific time in its history, it will enlighten anybody from any continent who wants to think through the issues that go to the heart of the family. By implication, we are confronted in these pages with the question ~ "What kind of culture do we want to pass on to our children?" Legally endorsing abortion would have serious implications for the individual and society. The author addresses the relevant topics in a manner designed to foster ethical discussion in a broader debate. It comes at a crucial time in a nation's struggle for identity in a world that is beguiled by a culture of death.

This book is a compilation of 15 blogs written by Kieran Beville. These first appeared in September and October 2016 at http://kieranbeville.blogspot.ie/ under the name "Kieran Beville ~ Biblical Blogger" and at http://nibandnoggin.blogspot.ie/ under the name "Sentry" others were published at http://scratchynib.blogspot.ie/ under the name "Quirky Quill". As such they can be read as separate chapters. There may be an element of overlap but not to any significant extent. With the release of this publication, these blogs will no longer be available, but the interested reader will find other topics there that may be of interest.

Nobody has the "right" to choose something that is morally wrong. People have the "ability" to do that, but this does not make it right. Christian leaders have a duty to make this known. The "right to choose" mantra has become so embedded in the psyches of people that even Christians are confused. Rights must be balanced with responsibilities. All choices have both limits and consequences.

There is, undoubtedly, much more that can be said on the issue of abortion but this intentionally short book is designed to kick-start conversation rather than be an exhaustive treatise on the topic.

If you would like the author to speak to a group, he may be contacted by Email: bevillekieran@gmail.com

When Does Human Life Begin?

While experts remain at odds over the issue of when life begins, most agree it's sometime after work.

Not everyone will agree about when human life begins. Is it at the moment of conception when the molecules making up the DNA of the father and mother combine to create a human life that never existed before? Is it the first heartbeat at about six weeks? Is it the point of viability outside the womb at about 22 weeks onward. Whatever one's opinion about this might be one cannot say that an embryo is not life. Pro-abortionists (and I think this is a better term than "pro-choice") seem to think that the unborn child is not a human being or the mass of matter does not matter! An ultra-scan reveals an embryo in the shape of a human being, a heartbeat, movement and biological gender. To argue that a foetus is not a life is absurd and unscientific. Biological science asserts 4 empirical attributes of life ~ growth, reproduction, metabolism, and response to stimuli.[1] The science of embryology has shown that all of these are present at fertilization.[2]

Furthermore, the sciences of genetics and embryology have proven that the genetic composition of humans is formed during fertilization, and textbooks on molecular biology refer to this genetic material as the very basis of life itself. In accord with these facts, the medical textbook *Before We Are Born: Essentials of Embryology and Birth Defects* states, "The zygote and early embryo are living human organisms."

---

[1] http://medical-dictionary.thefreedictionary.com/Biological+life

[2] http://www.justfactsdaily.com/the-science-of-abortion-when-does-life-begin/

And an organism, in the words of Webster's College Dictionary is "any individual life form considered as an entity."[3] Modern science has also revealed that each human embryo is biologically unique. Is the embryo human or just a piece of tissue or a mass of protoplasm without rights? Some people seem to think that just because it is not self-sufficient outside the uterus it is a parasite with no right to live. Every characteristic the human will ever have is contained in the genes of the ovum and sperm as soon as united. Helmut Thielicke has said, "Once impregnation has taken place, it is no longer a question of whether the parents concerned have the responsibility for a possible parenthood; they have already become parents." Abortion is about people actively ending the lives of unborn children, let us be clear about that.

---

[3] Drs. Keith L. Moore, T.V.N. Persaud, and Mark G. Torchia, *Before We Are Born: Essentials of Embryology and Birth Defects*, Elsevier / Saunders; 8th edition, 2012.

Baby in a Bucket

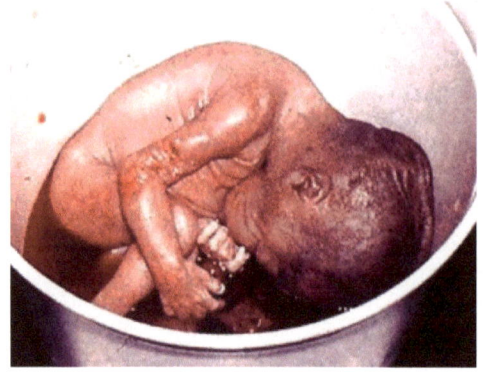

Amnesty International says this aborted baby has no rights. There are plenty of recorded testimonies from midwives and other medical professionals in maternity departments (what a misnomer) and abortion clinics who have seen babies who were born alive during abortions procedures but were left to die. I have read many of these testimonies. These horror stories are real and traumatic. I read about one student midwife who was 19 years old when she had an internship in the maternity department of a hospital in France. She witnessed babies being left alone to die, struggling to breathe and crying. She said, "The lucky ones are born dead."

Many medical practitioners are uncomfortable about leaving babies to die or killing them by lethal injection once they have been born alive during an abortion. Some are afraid of not having their contracts renewed.

The reality of what happens during an abortion is shocking, and people in these death chambers conceal the truth from women having abortions. I read about a baby boy who was born alive. To prevent it from crying, the doctor quickly covered the baby's face. The baby was then taken to resuscitation room (another misnomer). There was no apparent defect; he was breathing and moving. He was fully formed, had eyelashes, hair, nails. The doctor came in and asked if he was still breathing. When he was told that the baby was alive, he said he would "resolve" (interesting euphemism) this with an injection. When the nurse asked if there was something more humane that could be done, he said he would prefer not to let the child suffer! How nice of him to be so merciful. He then pierced the baby in the heart and injected the product. During the injection, the child moved all its members indicating that he suffered. The doctor performing the abortion clearly did not want the baby boy to cry because he thought it would be too traumatic for the mother. This is cold-blooded killing. Is this what we want in Ireland? Say "No" to abortion.

Stop the Torture and Killing of Unborn Children Coming to Ireland

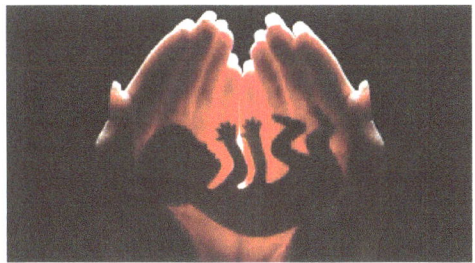

Babies born alive during late-term abortions must be given proper medical treatment as a basic human right. They should be given the same degree of care as any other baby born prematurely at the same age.[4]

Methods of abortion should also be investigated. Sometimes the baby is killed by lethal injection in the heart and then the birth is induced. Sometimes this injection is badly done or does not produce the desired effect, and the child is born alive. The most common method of late abortion is dilatation-evacuation whereby the cervix is dilated then the "content of the uterus" (interesting phrase) is pulled out with a clamp. In the end, the pieces are examined to make sure everything has been removed. This means that the body is gathered like a puzzle because in many cases, it has been dismembered during the operation. If there was no foeticide injection first or if the injection did not cause death the foetus was alive while its members were being torn off one after the other. This terribly cruel method is inhumane and constitutes torture.

Since 2007, there has been substantial medical research undertaken that has changed the way in which the medical community should view the ability of an unborn child of 20 weeks or younger to experience pain. Those that argue that the foetus is incapable of feeling pain before 29 to 30 weeks of development base their argument on 3 factors: (1) the requirement of a functioning cortex, or connections from the periphery to the cortex, in order to experience pain. This functioning of the cortex is argued not to occur until 23 to 24 weeks. (2) The behavioural reactions of premature infants to pain can be stimulated without pain and therefore is not evidence of the infant experiencing pain and (3) no evidence that premature infants can remember and interpret pain like an adult.

---

[4] I want to make it absolutely clear that I do not favour any form of abortion unless it is necessary to save the life of the mother. I will post blogs about hard cases later.

There have been several studies conducted that directly contradict this understanding. One of the most prominent was conducted by Dr K.J.S. Anand who is one of the key experts in this field. I read his findings ~ very technical language and not suited to a general blog but the findings are unmistakable ~ foetuses and neonates can feel pain as much or more than adults. Many other doctors attest to this. Other scientific studies also show that the foetus is responsive to touch by 8 weeks and feels suffering by the 14th week. At 20 weeks s/he has the physical structures necessary to experience pain. Researchers have observed that the foetus reacts to intrahepatic (within the liver) vein needling with vigorous body and breathing movements. In the U.S.A. the medical community now has the prevailing view that current knowledge suggests that humane considerations should apply to the foetus.

Not only are there biological indicators that pain can and is experienced by premature infants before 20 weeks, but also other factors such as cardiorespiratory changes in heart rate and blood pressure in response to painful stimuli, hormonal and metabolic changes in reaction to stress, and motor responses such as moving limbs, crying, grimacing, etc. A motor response can first be seen as a whole body movement away from a stimulus and observed on ultrasound from as early as 7.5 weeks' gestational age. The perioral area (tissue around the mouth) is the first part of the body to respond to touch at approximately 8 weeks, but by 14 weeks most of the body is responsive to touch." Many doctors who administer anaesthesia before performing surgery on infants in the womb attest that premature infants have the ability to experience pain. In light of much research recognizing an infant's ability to feel pain by 20 weeks, why are children in the womb treated with such callous cruelty?

Should the 8th Amendment be Repealed?

The Eighth Amendment of the Constitution of Ireland Act, 1983 introduced a ban on abortion by recognising the right to life of an unborn child. It was approved by referendum on 7 September 1983 and signed into law on the 7 October of the same year. After a rancorous referendum campaign, the amendment was passed by 67% voting in favour to 33% voting against.

Intense Focus

There is now an intense focus on repealing the 8th Amendment with an orchestrated and well-funded campaign underway. Discussion has taken place in the Dáil about the issue of "fatal foetal abnormality," which was initially mooted on the basis of "foetal abnormality." This change was a thinly disguised strategic manoeuvre to drive the sharp end of the wedge into this issue rather than the blunt end, where abortions could be performed on the basis of *any* abnormality. Thus it reveals the true agenda and ultimate end of the pro-choice lobby. This is happening in the UK and other constituencies where babies with defects like Down's syndrome and cleft palette are being aborted.

Lessons from Other Countries

The 1966 UK Abortion Act allowed for abortion in limited circumstances, such as medical reasons. It envisaged that therapeutic abortion would be a side effect of the medical treatment of the mother. But now abortion on demand is the reality and the norm, whatever the small print might say. Only a tiny proportion of the abortions performed are for legitimate "medical" reasons. The vast majority is for social reasons and come into the category of late birth control.

Principle and Pragmatism

I favour abortion to save the life of the mother; it is an abortion without any medical justification that I oppose. The concern I share with many others is that legislating for this could be a slippery slope and that whatever safeguards are initially put in place will eventually be removed or ignored. We have seen in countries where abortion, euthanasia, and assisted suicide are permitted that once the principle has been conceded amoral pragmatism takes the ascendancy. Like many other Christians, I'm trying to work through this issue in order to bring a Christian perspective to into focus for myself and others.

Political Moves

Ruth Coppinger TD moved a Bill, unopposed (on behalf of Anti-Austerity Alliance and People before Profit) for a referendum to repeal the 8th Amendment on 30th June, 2016. She expressed the need for all pro-choice activists, campaigners, and groups to use the next 100 days to contact their TDs, arrange to meet them and discuss with them why they should vote in favour of this Bill.[5]

Pro-choice Rallies

The annual "March for Choice" took place last Saturday in Dublin (24th September 2016). Busloads of people were transported from all over the country to attend that rally. Earlier this year the Project Arts Theatre (Dublin) was forced to paint over a repeal mural – and that mural was projected on to Cork School of Music.

A Pro-Choice public meeting was held in Cork on 31 August (at Isaacs Hotel). I'm sure that many other such meetings have already taken place in other parts of the country and that many more meetings and rallies will take place in the near future. The speakers at the Cork meeting were author Ailbhe Smyth (Coalition to Repeal the Eighth Amendment and founder and former director of Women's Studies in UCD), Mary Favier (Doctors for Choice) and Fiona Ryan (Anti-Austerity Alliance Councillor for Cork City North-Central, ROSA).[6]

Being Visible and Vocal

A referendum on this issue is very likely to take place in the not-too-distant future. If that was to happen tomorrow, I believe (on the basis of recent opinion polls) that the 1983 result would be reversed in a mirror image in percentage terms. I am concerned that the evangelical Christian community is neither visible nor vocal on this issue. I have not seen any statement from Christian denominations on this crucial social and moral issue. I am not aware that associations representing non-denominational, independent evangelical churches have any statements, position papers or policies, yet.

---

[5] Here is a link (3 minutes) to her speech: https://www.youtube.com/watch?v=-4t4pcZKZzw

[6] ROSA (for Reproductive rights, against oppression, Sexism & Austerity) has been initiated by women in the Socialist Party, with the aim of promoting and organising events, actions and campaigning activity on reproductive rights, against oppression, sexism and austerity. It's named after Rosa Parks, the inspirational black campaigner who famously refused to give up her seat for a white passenger, sparking the Montgomery bus boycott of the Civil Rights Movement. And also after Rosa Luxemburg, exceptional and leading socialist theoretician and activist of the early 20th century, killed for her revolutionary politics in 1919.

Repeal the 8th?

Should the 8th amendment be repealed? I'm not going to answer that question now (sorry to disappoint) but I do intend to address it later (watch this space). Right now I would like to know if there is sufficient interest to organise a meeting to discuss this. A necessary first step in a strategic approach to a possible campaign would be to hold a meeting where we could be briefed on the matter and have concerns addressed. This would involve a presentation of the arguments for and against and a Q & A session. But I should clarify that I am not interested in debating with pro-choice advocates and neither am I interested in a public forum. My aim and hope is to help Christians become informed and to think through the relevant issues. I am willing to do this (in Cork or anywhere else) if there is an appetite for it.

Abortion Coming to Ireland?

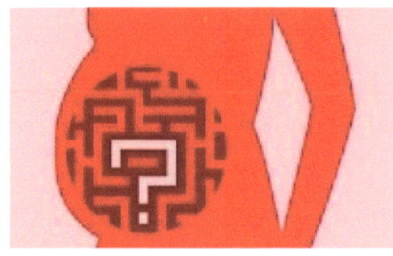

The pro-choice slogan "Repeal the 8th" is seriously flawed and those who campaign for that might have to settle for "reform" or "replacement" instead of repeal. A repeal of the 8th would lead to abortion on demand, without any medical "justification" or term limits. In reality, this means that a perfectly healthy baby could be killed up to the time of birth, simply because it is unwanted. I wonder if that is what all pro-choice activists really want. Perhaps some of the more militant among them desire this but I suspect there are some who do not.

Restrictions

Leo Varadkar (former Minister for Health, now Minister for Social Protection) is on record saying that term limits for abortion should be considered in the event of the eighth amendment to the Constitution being repealed. Likewise the Taoseach, Enda Kenny has also expressed the view that most pro-choice people want restrictions to choice in this matter.

Citizen's Assembly

There is now a Citizens' Assembly that will discuss a possible change to the legal ban on abortion. They will meet in Dublin Castle October 15th. The assembly consists of 100 members and will be chaired by Supreme Court judge Mary Laffoy. The other 99 members have been selected by pollsters Red C and will be representative of the electorate in terms of gender, age and geography. Potential members were not asked their views on the issue of abortion. So the Eighth Amendment to the Constitution which underpins Ireland's abortion laws is now coming under scrutiny. Red C has also been asked to select a panel of 99 substitute members. This selection process is underway. The names of assembly members will be made public, though not their addresses, as was the case with the constitutional convention held by the last Government. The proceedings of the assembly will be broadcast live on the internet. Incidentally, it should be noted that the pro-choice campaign sees the Citizen's Assembly as a stalling mechanism and are demanding abortion rights, now!

What Next?

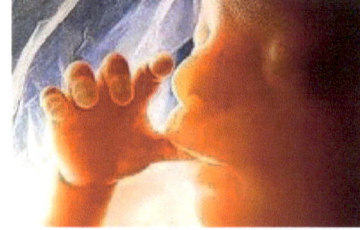

The assembly will discuss the future of the constitutional ban on abortion in several sessions over the coming months, probably seeking submissions and input from interested groups and relevant experts. It will then submit a report to the Oireachtas. It is likely that the report will be finalised in the first half of 2017.

The report will then go to an Oireachtas committee which may hold hearings before making its recommendations to the Government. Any proposal to either repeal or replace article 40.3.3 would have to be passed by the Dáil and ultimately put to the people in a referendum.

Opinion and Expectations

Pro-choice supporters say there is a gathering momentum for a change in Ireland's abortion laws following a large turnout at the recent (24th Sept., 2016) "March for Choice" in Dublin. Anti-abortion campaigners have pointed to a large rally in June (2016) in support of the Eighth Amendment.

Currently, the 8th Amendment guarantees the equal right to life of the mother and the unborn child. I think there is probably a consensus to have the abortion laws liberalised, but not without restrictions. We can expect opinion polls to be conducted over the coming months to gauge consensus for a change on abortion. No doubt these will feed into the Citizen's Assembly's remit to consider the matter. So we can expect "conversations" about abortion to take place on radio and TV programmes and in other public forums.

Mood Music

The government has resisted pressure for an early referendum and is committed to a consultative process before any decision is taken on how to proceed. Thus we now have a judge-led assembly to examine the issue.

Recently the UN Human Rights Committee demanded that the constitutional ban on abortion in Ireland be rescinded. Although there are many independent voices in the Dáil pushing for repeal of the 8th it should be noted that the mood in Fianna Fáil and Fine Gael is to proceed with caution. Both parties intend to allow their TDs and Senators to have a free vote on abortion law if it comes before the Oireachtas.

Abortion: Unmasking the Liberal Agenda in Ireland

Recently the story of a woman who travelled to England (Amanda Mellet) for an abortion (2011) when her foetus was diagnosed with a fatal foetal abnormality has caught the public imagination. It has been reported that she "had to go to England for an abortion."[7] She spent 36 hours in labour.[8] Still weak and bleeding she travelled back to Dublin within hours of the birth because she could not afford to stay in the U.K. Why did not one of the many well-funded organisations campaigning for "Repeal the 8th" come to her aid and pay for her care and accommodation in the U.K. if they were so concerned and outraged by her plight? The answer is that "horror stories" suit their agenda and this is evidenced in their contextualising and highlighting the case in a manner that attracted much biased publicity and negative international attention.

The pro-choice movement want abortion on demand, without restrictions and they are on record insisting on this (see below). They are happy to use this woman's case to achieve that end. But make no mistake about it they will not be content with any law that permits abortion in limited circumstances such as fatal foetal abnormality, rape, incest etc.

Callous and Cruel

At the risk of being branded callous and cruel I must say that there are other peculiarities in this story that need to be addressed. Everybody has sympathy and compassion for any woman who finds herself in this position. But she is a pawn in a broader campaign to liberalise abortion laws in Ireland (perhaps a willing participant in that battle, I don't know).

There was another option. She could have given birth to the baby, named it and had a funeral to mark the sad passing of her child. I think this would have been better for the woman in the long run and more dignified and less traumatic.

---

[7] Jacky Jones, "Vindicating Women's Rights Does Not Lead to Chaos", *Irish Times*, 21 June, 2016.

[8] A method of abortion for late term gestation is to induce labour and then drown the birthed infant in water or formaldehyde or leave it to die of exposure in a bin or on a steel tray or put it in a freezer. This is often a viable foetus who could survive if given care (many breathe, cry and move for a long time). But in this instance we are informed that the baby had a fatal abnormality, which means it could not survive outside the womb. Usually they are either disposed in a furnace or harvested for parts. But in this instance Amanda Mellet received her daughter's ashes by courier a few weeks later.

It is natural for a woman to give birth. It is not natural for a mother to kill her child and doing so can lead to guilt, shame, and psychological trauma that can have repercussions throughout her life. It should be clearly stated here that an abortion does not make a woman "un-pregnant" rather it makes her the mother of a dead child. Of course, I will be lambasted for not accepting her choice or her right to make that decision for herself. In reality, she was not denied choice but there were restrictions on that choice and no possibility of exercising it in Ireland, legally, which is at the core of the issue. But I think it shows a callousness and cruelty on the part of the pro-choice campaigners to pretend they are fighting for the rights of women in such circumstances when the reality is otherwise.

If Article 40.3.3 is removed by referendum, then any subsequent legislation that seeks some protection for the unborn is subject to challenge in the courts, on the basis that the people wanted such protection removed outright. Therefore, any pro-life government initiative is likely to be struck down. The repeal campaign has possibly been briefed on this and that might explain the push for complete repeal.

UNHRC Rebuke

The United Nations Human Rights Committee (UNHRC) found she had been subjected to cruel, inhuman, and degrading treatment in violation of article seven of the International Covenant on Civil and Political Rights. They also found that her rights in relation to article 17 (privacy) and article 26 (discrimination) had been violated. The committee called on Ireland to amend its laws to ensure "effective, timely and accessible procedures for pregnancy termination in Ireland." The State has 180 days (until December 6th) to supply "information about the measures taken to give effect to the committee's views." Incidentally, there is no "human right" to abortion in the UN founding documents, and so Ireland already is in compliance.

Being Lectured

We are being lectured now by many inside and outside Ireland who assert that "In the past, Ireland's extremely restrictive abortion laws did not ensure babies and children had their human rights respected. If anything, society's censorious attitudes to sex and the so-called pro-life stance produced a culture in which Magdalene laundries, mother-and-baby homes, and illegal adoptions flourished."[9] But the problem with that argument is that those days are gone and the stigma attached then to unwed mothers has disappeared. So, logically, to use this as an argument for the necessity to legitimise abortion, is irrational. But that is the kind of absurdity we can expect as this debate progresses. This same pro-abortion champion has said,

---

[9] Jacky Jones, "Vindicating Women's Rights Does Not Lead to Chaos", *Irish Times*, 21 June, 2016.

"Even countries with abysmal track records on women's rights such as Iran, India, and Turkey allow abortion in cases of foetal impairment."[10] Again the logic is flawed as abortion is itself a breach of human rights. So, why would governments which care little about human rights not have legislation to permit abortion in their countries?

We are constantly being told that to oppose the introduction of abortion legislation is to deny women their human rights. But what about the human rights of the unborn child? I don't hear the UNHRC or Amnesty International raising a hue and cry about this. How can it be that a woman's right to choose trumps the life of a child? We should make no mistake about this ~ the campaign to introduce abortion to Ireland is a well-funded, international crusade by aggressive atheists, militant secularists, the LGBT community and radical feminist elements. This is evident from those attending these rallies. Many lesbians, who do not intend to give birth, are on the front lines, including Katherine Zappone, Ireland's first openly lesbian government minister and the first minister to have been openly gay at the time of first appointment to cabinet, when Enda Kenny chose her as the Minister for Children and Youth Affairs. Yes, the LGBT community has a right to comment and protest like everybody else but it seems odd that a group of people who are so removed from fertility issues (most lesbians do not intend to conceive) should be leading this cause.

Time for Change

We are being told it is time for change and that those who do not want the introduction of abortion in this country are out of touch with Irish and international public opinion on this issue. Pro-choice lobbyists are advocating for a modern maternity strategy that includes abortion services. Does this not seem bizarre? So your taxes could well be directed into abortion funding.

Zappone (an American-born feminist theologian and independent politician) was at the recent "Pro-Choice rally in Merrion Square wearing a Repeal sweatshirt and actively backing the repeal drive. She called for a wider discussion on abortion beyond cases of fatal foetal abnormalities, rape and incest and clearly expressed the view that she favours abortion not only for these hard cases but a much more permissive availability of abortion. The mask slipped just enough for those who might not have known how ugly her intentions are to get a glimpse of the real persona of Ireland's Minister for Children and Youth Affairs.

Have they become over-confident? If there is a proposed *reform* of the 8th (setting out limits and allowing for abortion for "hard cases") rather than an outright *repeal* it is likely the electorate will vote in favour of that. However, if

---

[10] Jacky Jones, "Vindicating Women's Rights Does Not Lead to Chaos", *Irish Times*, 21 June, 2016.

voters are made aware of the real agenda (to have abortion on demand, without limits) the pro-life side could win. Pro-choice campaigners are now openly saying what they want and it is very permissive. Their thinking now seems to be that nothing but repeal will comply with international human rights' rulings. Thus they are looking for the complete dismantling of protection for the unborn. I'm not sure if the pro-choice camp has made a *faux pas* by insisting on full repeal or whether they think this is the best way for them to succeed. I tend to see it as a strategic error of judgement on their part because it will be difficult to win hearts and minds by pushing for abortion without limits.

This, like same-sex marriage, is another battle in a clash of cultures where people with conservative values and those advocating a liberal agenda will slog it out. I have no interest in fighting this battle and will refuse to engage in futile polemics with pro-choice militants. My only concern is to ensure that those who are pro-life are well informed on this issue and perhaps that those who are undecided might be persuaded to do the right thing and protect the rights of unborn children.

Amnesty International want Permissive Abortion in Ireland

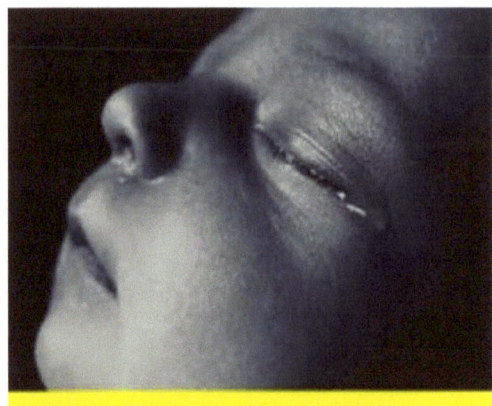

AMNESTY USED TO BE A VOICE FOR THE VOICELESS. NOW THEY WANT TO KILL THEM

Writing in the *Irish Times* (7 July 2016) Colm O' Gorman (Executive Director of Amnesty International, Ireland) expressed the view that public support for greater abortion access is overwhelming. Is that wishful thinking?

He cites a national Red C poll conducted in February 2016 on attitudes to abortion which found that 87% of people want expanded access to abortion. But that was before the pro-choice campaign vocalised their demand for abortion extended beyond "hard cases." I doubt that there would be such a consensus for the kind of unrestricted abortion that Amnesty desire. I honestly believe the Irish people will not vote for that.

He said that the Eighth Amendment needs to be removed from the Irish Constitution and that a legal and healthcare framework should be put in place that respects women's and girls' rights. What about girls in the womb, will they have their human rights respected? I used to love the work of Amnesty International but now that they advocate for abortion I have lost respect for that organisation, and I suspect I am not alone in this. There are possibly thousands of people in Ireland alone who cannot subscribe to their warped political agenda. Perhaps it is time for a new organisation to champion human rights, including the right to life of the unborn. It is mind-boggling that Amnesty does not champion the human rights of unborn children. It is astonishing that a single cell form of life found on another planet is celebrated and protected, but an infant in the womb on this planet may be deemed not worthy of protection.

O' Gorman cites the case of Amanda Mellet who had been denied an abortion in Ireland in 2011. She was subsequently represented by the New York-based Center for Reproductive Rights in a complaint lodged with the UN Human Rights Committee arguing that Ireland's restrictive abortion laws violated her human rights. Ms. Mellet and others like her have become very effective advocates for the pro-abortion campaign. Telling their harrowing stories and engaging people at an emotional level.

The committee reported that Ireland's laws prohibiting abortion subjected Amanda to "intense physical and mental suffering." It must have been a very distressing time for her, but she could have had a lot of support in Ireland if she decided to give birth here. The committee found that Ireland's criminalisation of abortion caused her shame and stigma. But the only stigma attached to this woman arises out of the shameful act of terminating the life of her daughter and this she brought upon herself. It is not Ms. Mellet that was subjected to cruel, inhuman or degrading treatment but her child. The committee also found that her right to privacy was violated, but surely it was only dishonoured by her.

The fact of the matter is that women in Ireland who continue with their pregnancies after a fatal foetal impairment diagnosis receive public health care and health insurance cover and Ms. Mellet could have availed of this but chose not to. She did not need to bear the full financial, emotional and physical burden at all. Hers was a very sad case, but she chose a path that made a difficult situation into an ordeal.

Now the UN committee is lecturing Ireland saying that the government must act swiftly and effectively to redress this issue by reforming its laws

In June 2016 Mick Wallace TD introduced a Dáil Bill to permit abortion in cases of fatal foetal abnormalities. During a debate on that Bill, Simon Harris, Minister for Health, offered a sincere apology to Ms. Mellet. Is that appropriate? Our Constitution forbids abortion, except to save the life of the mother and the mother's life in this instance was not under threat. This apology has been hailed as an important moment by those seeking change. O' Gorman expressed the hope that the government accepts the UN findings and called on them to act upon it without equivocation.

The right to life of an unborn child is enshrined in the Irish Constitution. If it is removed hundreds of thousands of unborn children will be aborted, not just in "hard cases" but perfectly healthy children will be killed. This is what is happening in other jurisdictions. This is a fact and it is what the pro-choice lobby want. They are actually calling for this.

O' Gorman said, "The purpose of international human rights law - a system of treaties and supervisory committees created by states, including Ireland - is to ensure that all people are afforded a minimum level of protection of a defined set of human rights. These human rights supersede domestic laws, which are often based on ideologies and prejudices. Therefore, respect for human rights can never be subject to the vagaries of public opinion or politics. And a state's constitution can never be an excuse for human rights abuses." This is stupendously ignorant of the fact that an unborn child is a human being. He actually expresses contempt for the will of the Irish people as enshrined in the 8th Amendment. He describes the democratic will of the Irish people, as expressed in 1983 as "the vagaries of public opinion." In doing this he is accusing those who exercised their views in a democratic process as whimsical and capricious. He holds the views of the Irish people in utter contempt. Are we to disregard the democratic will of the people of Ireland? Is it only the democratic will of the people when it conforms to O' Gorman's view? He seems to think that his views fall outside the scope of ideology and prejudice but they certainly do not because his view is ideologically driven and highly prejudicial. The Constitution is designed to protect us from the whims of politicians and in that regard on this issue it has served the Irish nation very well indeed.

O' Gorman says, "Too often discussion of abortion is derailed by aggressive and personalised condemnation of those seeking progress." The reality is that there has been "aggressive and personalised condemnation" from both sides and the pro-choice group are not innocent victims as Amnesty would have us believe. His notion of "progress" is twisted. He goes on to say that, "This approach serves only those who want to close down public discussion and maintain the status quo." He seems to think that voices which dissent from the liberal orthodoxy are a nuisance. There are plenty of pro-life people who are more than willing to have a public discussion on this issue. Rather it is O' Gorman's views that are censorious. He would like the pro-life people to shut up and go away. I thought Amnesty championed the right to free speech but it seems they only do that if they like what you are saying. That is not actually free speech ~ that is political correctness. George Orwell said, "If liberty means anything at all it means the right to tell people what they do not want to hear." I do not think balance in the media is best served by insisting that every article must be even-handed in presenting both sides of this debate. Rather there should be equal proportion in the number of articles presenting diverse opinions and we are a long way from that ideal. To quote Orwell again, "During times of universal deceit, telling the truth becomes a revolutionary act."

Furthermore, he says, "Imagine you are a journalist trying to do your job, objectively and responsibly, but you know that every word is pored over looking for an opportunity to charge bias, and the inevitable deluge of abuse." The problem is that there has been media bias and some journalists are subjective and irresponsible. The tenor of his article suggests that he wants his/Amnesty's views not to be critiqued and challenged. He seems to want his/Amnesty's views to go unscrutinised and uncontested. If he had his way the public would be subjected to a diet of propaganda on the abortion issue and anyone who thinks otherwise would be gagged. Voltaire said, "To learn who rules over you, simply find out who you are not allowed to criticize." The greatest human rights violation today is abortion. This is in many places a silent holocaust, and it is shameful that Amnesty International will not defend unborn children.

Amnesty do not like the fact that a citizens' assembly has been appointed to consider the Eighth Amendment and they are lecturing the government that, "it must mandate the assembly to expand access to abortion, not maintain the status quo." Clearly, he is cynical about this initiative. If Amnesty supports the death penalty for unborn children, it's time to abandon Amnesty International. I cannot support this organisation because it has failed in their mandate and mission to defend the human rights of unborn children.

Blackadder ~ Ireland's Minister for Children and Abortion

The healthcare system in Ireland does not ignore (as has been stated in the media) women who receive a fatal foetal abnormality diagnosis. Those who continue with their pregnancies can avail of public healthcare and health insurance. There is no need to bear the financial, emotional and physical burden of travelling to the UK for an abortion. That is a path that makes a difficult situation into an ordeal.

According to the master of the Rotunda Hospital, 49 women made the decision to travel to the UK for abortions in 2015. A total of 71 cases were diagnosed. Is it desirable that Ireland should introduce permissive abortion (i.e. abortion for social reasons rather than medical reasons) whereby thousands of unborn infants are killed, on the basis of such hard cases? I think not. Opinion and analysis pieces in our newspapers have shown bias in favour of abortion being introduced to Ireland.

Abortion on demand would be the legal outcome of the repeal of the Eighth Amendment. Simply removing protection for the unborn opens the way to unlimited abortion. The common good will not be well served by this.

The most obvious interpretation of any decision to delete article 40.3.3 is that the people will have decided to withdraw constitutional protection from the unborn completely. Gerry White has said, "…the people voted for the amendment, thereby asserting their role as the ultimate arbiter of constitutional policy on abortion and precluding the Oireachtas and the courts from developing the law in this area other than in accordance with the terms of article 40.3.3."[11] That decision has saved the lives of thousands of unborn children in Ireland. But that was 33 years ago, and one wonders now if that decision will withstand the pressure to repeal. Ireland has changed a lot since 1983. The words of William Butler Yeats seem apt, "All changed, changed utterly/A terrible beauty is born."

The present constitutional position is that both the right to life of the mother and the unborn are protected and that the life of the mother prevails wherever continuation of the pregnancy poses a real and substantial risk to the mother's life. If the Eighth Amendment to the Constitution is repealed there will be no

---

[11] Gerry Whyte , "Abortion on demand the legal outcome of repeal of Eighth Amendment", *The Irish Times*, 28 Sept., 2016. Gerry Whyte lectures in law in Trinity College. In 2005, he dissented from the majority report of the Commission on Assisted Human Reproduction on the specific question of the legal protection that should be afforded to the embryo.

restriction on the mother's constitutional rights in relation to her decision to terminate her pregnancy and that would effectively mean abortion on demand.

It was reported in August this year (2016) that a Mr. Richard Humphreys (High Court judge) declared the rights of the unborn child meant the right to life and more. He said the unborn child, including the unborn child of a parent facing deportation, has significant rights and legal protection in common law, by statute, and under the Constitution, "going well beyond the right to life alone."[12]

He said article 42a of the Constitution, inserted as a result of the 2012 Children's Referendum, provides the State must protect "all" children. Because an "unborn" is "clearly a child," article 42a means all children "both before and after birth."

Yet we have the incredible spectacle of the Irish Minister for Children, Katherine Zappone, actively campaigning for permissive abortion, well beyond "hard cases." If it wasn't true and so serious it could make a hilarious comedy sketch in *Blackadder*.

These statements from High Court judge Mr Richard Humphreys were made in the context of the state seeking the deportation of a Nigerian, his partner and their now one-year-old child who was born after the case was initiated. I find it fascinating that one of the arguments in the Irish state's case was that "the only right the unborn child had was to life" (asserting it had no legal right to remain in Ireland) ~ hello ~ Katherine Zappone please take note!

The killing of unborn children will remain unethical irrespective of any constitutional change in Ireland.

---

[12] Mary Carolan, "'Unborn child' has significant legal rights, judge rules", *The Irish Times*, 2 Aug., 2016.

"Amnesty International" or "Damn Nasty International"

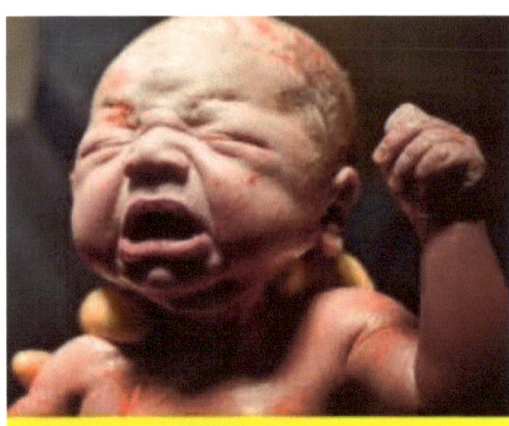

AMNESTY SUPPORT ABORTION UNTIL BIRTH

Why does the unborn child have no human rights? Amnesty International is supposed to be dedicated to the promotion and protection of human rights but not when it comes to the unborn child. When a child is born prematurely, everything is done to save him. If this is not possible, s/he receives comforting care and is supported until his death. Neonatal palliative care is well developed in many hospitals. The situation is different for those children who are born alive after an abortion. Children are often born alive due to a failed abortion after the 20th week of pregnancy. They are abandoned to die without care, struggling to breathe, sometimes for several hours, or they are killed by lethal injection or suffocation, and often thrown away with medical waste. Amnesty support abortion at 40 weeks gestation that is, up to the time of birth!

The method most often used to perform late abortions is called "dilation-evacuation," where the cervix is dilated to remove the baby with surgical pliers, which is very painful. The child is often extracted in pieces. Generally, pain-killer is not used for this. This act of foeticide does not register on Amnesty's radar ~ strange! There is plenty of reliable data and testimonies of medical practitioners who witnessed these practices, but Amnesty doesn't care.

According to the *British Journal of Obstetrics and Gynaecology*, at 23 weeks of pregnancy, 10% of children survive an attempted abortion. Leaving babies to die without treatment, or actively killing them, simply because they are not wanted is inhuman and contrary to fundamental rights. According to European law, all human beings born alive have the same right to life and to receive necessary treatment and care, irrespective of the circumstances of their birth.

It is time that Amnesty International was denounced for their indifference (indeed their support) for this. All right-minded, decent human beings are horrified by this. It's time to speak out boldly against this form of cruelty and to call for an end to these practices so that all newly born children are treated as human beings.

In terms of viability, it is possible to humanely improve this situation by developing excellent practices in neonatal care for the child. A premature baby, even born during an attempted late-term abortion, is a human being. Amnesty should be denouncing the torture, and infanticide inflicted on children born alive following an attempted late-term abortion. Numerous babies survive abortion. In these cases, they are left to die or are actively killed. These practices must be identified as serious violations of human rights.

When a child is born prematurely, medical practitioners make every effort to save the life of the baby. If survival is not possible, the baby still receives care and is supported until death. This conforms to the International Convention on the Rights of the Child which mandates that everything possible is done to ensure the survival and development of the child.[13]

With the advance of medicine, premature babies can be saved as early as 21 weeks, even before the limit of viability as defined by the World Health Organisation (22 weeks or 500g).[14]

Presently, abortion is free on demand until the 18th week in Sweden even if the sole reason for this abortion is the sex of the baby)[15] up to 24 weeks in the United Kingdom and the Netherlands. In some countries, such as France and the United Kingdom, abortions are performed up until birth in the case of a serious (but non-fatal) anomaly. For instance, in 2012, according to the official statistics of the United Kingdom, there had been four cases of abortion (before 24 weeks) because of a cleft lip or palette, 191 anomalies were of the cardiovascular system, many of which could have been treated by surgery, 149 were spina bifida, 5 of which were after the 24th week, and 544 were Down Syndrome, 3 of which were after the 24th week. It is clear, therefore, that abortions are permissible even if the foetus is viable and healthy.

Late term abortions are technically difficult to perform (at 20 weeks, the rate of complications is ten times higher than before 12 weeks according to the official statistics of the United Kingdom). Thus, it can occur that viable babies who were supposed to be aborted are born alive. After 21 weeks, some of those were able to breathe unaided for a long period of time.

When a pregnancy has reached its 16th week, the usual termination method employed is birth induction. In most cases, the heart of the baby stops during labour, and it is born dead. However, some babies survive this procedure, and the number of surviving babies increases as the pregnancy advances. Children are often born alive between the 22nd and the 24th weeks. Knowing this, medical

---

[13] See Art. 6 of the International Convention on the Rights of the Child.

[14] Note the case of Amilia, born in October 2006 in the Baptist Children's Hospital, Miami. She was born at 22 weeks of pregnancy and survived without future difficulties.

[15] In May 2009 Swedish health authorities ruled that gender-based abortion is legal.

practitioners often inject digoxin or potassium chloride into the foetal heart without anaesthetic. This stops the heart. An injection can also be given during delivery when the child is partially born. This has a high failure rate so that frequently the child is born alive.

Being born alive after an abortion is not exceptional. This problem occurs in all countries allowing late-term abortions. The hearts of some of the aborted children continued to beat for hours. In 2010 in Italy, a baby, who was aborted at 22 weeks because of a cleft palate, was discovered alive 20 hours after birth and continued to survive for one more day. In the Netherlands the situation is even worse: after 24 weeks, in cases of serious malformation, not only is abortion possible but so is infanticide (i.e. an infant's life may be terminated after it has come to full term and been born).[16] In France, children born before 22 weeks or during a medical termination of pregnancy have no birth certificate but only a record of a lifeless child, even if they were born alive. According to Article 79-1 of the Civil Code, "The record drawn up shall be without prejudice to knowing whether the child has lived or not." No information is given on the number of children born alive or how long they survive such procedures.

In the United Kingdom In 2005, the *British Journal of Obstetrics and Gynaecology* published the conclusions of Dr. Shantala Vadeyar, a researcher at the St. Mary Hospital (Manchester), who states that children at 18 weeks have survived, for a certain time, outside the uterus after an abortion. Dr. Vadeyar revealed that in the North West between 1996 and 2001, at least 31 children survived attempted abortions. In 2007, a study published in the *British Journal of Obstetrics and Gynaecology* concluded that around one abortion out of 30 beyond 16 weeks of pregnancy results in the birth a living child. At 23 weeks, the level of children born reached 9.7%.

One suspects that many botched abortions, where the child is born alive, are not reported, and thus the statistics are skewed. The mother usually does not want her baby to receive intensive care. One wonders how many would have had a reasonable chance of survival if they received appropriate care.

Oversight and reporting are problematic because of the taboo surrounding this and so we are left with witness testimonies about children abandoned without care while they struggle to breathe, sometimes injured by the abortion, before dying alone. Some are asphyxiated or thrown away with waste despite signs of

---

[16] The Groningen Protocol is a document dating from 2004 by Eduard Verhagen, the medical director of the department of paediatrics at the University Medical Centre Groningen (UMCG) in Groningen, the Netherlands. It contains directives with criteria under which physicians can perform "active ending of life on infants" (child euthanasia) without fear of legal prosecution.

life. In other words, these newborns are killed or left to die, even though in another room, doctors try to save premature babies of the same gestational age. What has Amnesty to say about that? Surely these are practices that violate human rights. Leaving newborns to die without care simply because they are unwanted is inhumane. Is this not torture and infanticide euphemistically re-designated?

These practices manifestly constitute blatant violations of universal human rights, notably the Convention on the Rights of the Child which declares, "…the child, by reason of his physical and mental immaturity, needs special safeguards and care, including appropriate legal protection, before as well as after birth." (Article 2). Killing infants or leaving them to die without care is also a blatant violation of the European Convention on Human Rights, in particular, their right to life (Article 2) and constitutes inhuman treatment (forbidden by Article 3 of the ECHR). These practices must be condemned and brought to an end. A premature baby born during an attempted late-term abortion is a human being. How can Amnesty International think that this does not come within its mandate? I'm renaming this organisation "Damn Nasty International" let's see if it takes off.

"A World Without Down's Syndrome" ~ A Review

On Wednesday, October 5th BBC 2 broadcast the documentary "A World Without Down's Syndrome." It was about the science and ethics behind screening for Down's syndrome (DS) during pregnancy. In this programme Sally Phillips (the mother of an 11-year-old boy named Olly who is DS) investigates a new, non-invasive, test offered by the NHS to diagnose Down's syndrome in utero. It was revealed (to all who might not have known) that in Iceland, the test has led to 100% of expectant mothers terminating their pregnancies when discovering Down's. In Denmark, it is 98%, and in the UK 90% of mothers terminate. The documentary (as the title suggests) raised the question of the possibility of a world without Down's syndrome.

Sally interviews mothers, doctors, geneticists, and those with Down's from around the world. What we discover through the documentary is truly disturbing ~ eugenics is alive and well and being practiced today.

In an article written before the documentary was aired Jane Fisher, Director of Antenatal Results and Choices, complains:

> Sally is a very compelling presenter, and – absolutely – it's great to have the positive images of people [with Down's] who are already here. But it's very personal, and it's an extra layer of difficulty for couples and families who might be making the decision now about whether to end their pregnancy. It risks offering the suggestion to those who have [decided to end a pregnancy] that they have made the wrong decision.[17]

In other words it is deemed to be unhelpful to have the other side presented in such a compelling way because people might be influenced to change their minds about terminating the pregnancy ~ So that's what Fisher means by "choice", the mask slipped but it's interesting to know what a person in her position really thinks. You can put your mask back on now Jane and pretend to the world that you support choice.

At one point Sally interviews Lynn Chitty, professor of genetics and foetal medicine, and asks her about the cost of the test. Sally is talking about the high

---

[17] Tracy McVeigh, "Sally Phillips's film on Down's is 'unhelpful' for families, warns antenatal specialist", *The Guardian*, 2 Oct., 2016.

cost to society of, potentially, eliminating people with DS but Jane responds by talking about financial costs and how affordable it is. Sally then clarifies that she was not asking about the financial cost but about "an experiment...that may result in catastrophic results for the Down's syndrome population." Frankly, it was chilling.

The underlying assumption of some people interviewed is that society should not be burdened by the vulnerable. Lynn then asks Sally, "How do you feel about later on in life? Because Olly is likely to outlive you, how do you feel about that prospect?" Sally responds, "The answer to that is not termination. The answer is that if we have a society that is unable to care for people, the problem is not the person." Here is a mother with a vulnerable child who is subjected to a question that suggests she would have been wiser to have had an abortion ~ cold, callous and cruel.

Are Lynn's views typical? If so this indicates a radical change in morality. A mother of a vulnerable child needs the support of a caring community. I spoke to somebody recently who told me she was discussing this documentary with an acquaintance and that this person said, "It is almost eradicated." She was referring to DS as a disease. But DS is not a disease rather it is a type of person with a different chromosome configuration.

There seems to be an assumption that life ought to be free from pain and problems. But suffering is part of life. Suffering should elicit compassion. Sally interviews Kate who decided to have an abortion at 25 weeks when she received a diagnosis of DS. Kate said she had investigated the matter by looking at You Tube videos and she talked about, "One woman whose 5-year-old son still wasn't walking... he was very heavy, having fits everywhere. If my child was affected as much as he was, I'd feel really guilty about that, having been given the choice." Here is misguided mercy. The vast majority of DS are very happy and bring a lot of joy to their families and is an enriching experience. It seems Kate trawled the internet for anecdotal material that would support her pre-determined decision. The overwhelming evidence is that DS children are happy and healthy and so too are their families, despite the challenges.

It seems that we now live in a society where we have to contend that human life is intrinsically valuable as it is no longer generally accepted as true. We seem to have drifted away from the understanding that life is sacred.

Sally interviews geneticist George Church (the "Godfather of Genetics" at Harvard University) a pioneer of genetic testing in utero. He advises Sally to educate people that those with Down's syndrome are valuable members of society. But is there not something seriously wrong with a society that does not know that? People like Sally Phillips will find herself arguing the case for people with DS ~ that they can be educated and achieve great things in many fields, such as sport and the arts, etc. But underlying this is a problem with a society that

needs to justify the existence of the life of someone with DS. Where will this lead?

There is clear bias in the way *The Guardian* discussed this documentary. Prior to screening, they cautioned that Phillips might upset mothers with her convincing approach to celebrating DS. Then after the documentary (6 October 2016) there was a review by Julia Raeside, "It's straight from the heart ~ and that's the problem." Raeside says it's "impassioned but not impartial." I find it odd that this documentary should be critiqued in this way. Our newspapers are filled with opinion and analysis pieces. It is not necessary for a documentary to present both sides of an issue. Balance is served by having different documentaries that present diverse views and this programme should be welcomed on that basis. In my opinion, it deserves to win a BAFTA award because it has made a distinctive and original contribution to this issue of screening out DS people from our world. But I would wager that she will be overlooked by the politically correct powers.

What was it that Raeside did not like about the programme? Was it Sally's happy family life that runs counter to the prevailing narrative that having a DS child is a disaster that can be avoided by termination? Was she offended by the reality of Olly's healthy and joyous demeanour? Or was it the portrayal of the inspirational achievements of those with Down's syndrome? Raeside and others like her need to know that this is not an issue that is about negative clinical data that emphasises problems and one-sided statistics that lists symptoms. That is not information: that is propaganda, and it feeds into directive counselling rather than presenting options and "choice." Where are the leaflets in the NHS celebrating DS and the stories of those who love their DS children?

I got the distinct impression from this programme that those who profess to value "choice" did not like Sally Phillips' choice. It seems to be an embarrassment. People with DS are people! They deserve our love and support and a documentary that takes an empathetic approach is worthy of honour. I thought it was beautiful, honest, sad, challenging and chilling. Sally Phillips came

across as a very capable and caring person with a gentle spirit. Yes she was pro-choice but as the documentary progressed she raised the question as to whether "choice" is always good. Phillips has done society a great service in confronting a culture of death. Dietrich Bonhoeffer said, "Silence in the face of evil is itself evil: God will not hold us guiltless. Not to speak is to speak. Not to act is to act." We cannot be complacent.

Abortion in Cases of Rape

Pregnancy resulting from rape or incest is undoubtedly tragic. One would have to have a heart of stone not to feel compassion for any woman in such a situation. What is the correct pastoral approach to such a difficult circumstance? As in all pastoral situations, we should be guided by grace and truth. The guiding *principle* is that the sanctity of human life is paramount and abortion is morally wrong. Therefore two wrongs don't make a right. From a *pragmatic* point of view, I think the problem would be compounded for an expecting mother by destroying the baby who is half her own DNA. Any woman who finds herself in this situation needs to be lavished with love, and nothing should be spared in helping her to find hope after the horror she has endured.

In the case of rape, the unborn child is innocent and should not receive the death penalty for a crime it did not commit. Even the perpetrator of such a horrendous crime would not be subjected to such a sentence in Western society.

Throughout history pregnant women sentenced to die were given a stay of execution until the child was born. The position of the courts was that the child should not be punished for the crime of the mother.

Even if abortion is allowed in the case of rape what is stopping a woman who gets pregnant from voluntary sexual intercourse claiming she was raped in order to procure an abortion. There are reasons why a woman might be tempted to do this, such as an adulterous relationship.

When rape has occurred, the victim should be promptly treated with vaginal irrigations and spermicides to prevent conception, and antibiotics should be given to prevent infection. Counselling and comfort must be doled out in abundance.

Pregnancy from rape is uncommon. Pregnancy rarely occurs from a single act of intercourse even with consenting couples. In rape, pregnancy is unlikely because of stress. I do not deny that it happens but it is a statistically rare problem which is being used to manipulate people into an agenda that explicitly desires abortion on demand, and as such it is disingenuous.

Rapists must be severely punished. Victims must be supported. But we must also tackle the issues contributing to this social evil, namely the lack of wholesome sex education and the need for strict laws banning all forms of pornography. In our permissive society, people want the liberty to have access to sexually explicit material that dehumanises and degrades women but then wring their hands in despair because the streets are not safe for women. You can't have it both ways or if you do there are serious consequences. I'm not saying there would not be any rape without pornography. History, including biblical history, records such vile incidents. However, I think it is a contributory factor to the prevalence of sexual violence today.

As in all pastoral situations, we can advise, comfort, challenge and refer, where necessary. Thus, we *counsel*. What we cannot do (and indeed would never want to do) is *coerce* a vulnerable person into a course of action against her will.

Abortion in cases of foetal abnormalities

First of all, I want to clarify that I have addressed the issue of "fatal" foetal abnormality in my blog, "Abortion: Unmasking the Liberal Agenda in Ireland." However, on the issue of abortion on the basis of foetal abnormalities there is something I want to say, hence this short blog. There is no evidence to suggest that babies with congenital defects would rather not be born. In fact, suicides are uncommon among people with physical disabilities or congenital anomalies. These people seem to value life. Suicide among this group is less than that of the general population.

Abortions are not performed for the sake of the foetus ~ that is a lie. Therapeutic abortion is not therapeutic for the baby! Abortion is a negative approach to foetal problems. If we decide to kill unborn children because of impairment what does that say to those already born and living with such impairment? Should we kill them also? What message are we giving to the blind and the deaf and the lame...?

Because some people are no longer self-sufficient, like the child in the womb, should they be euthanized? This attitude has serious implications for the ill and elderly. One author has said, "And if the doctor, the mother, and the legislator can combine in their judgment to decide that a baby is not to live, then who in turn is to decide when the mother, the doctor, or the legislator may not live?"[18]

Once you allow the killing of unborn children there will be no stopping the slide into infanticide, assisted suicide and euthanasia. It is all part of the same culture of death. Let the Christian voice be united and heard extolling the value of life as a gift from God (Psalm 127:3) that should be celebrated not terminated.

---

[18] John Grady, *Abortion: Yes or No?*, 1967, 1979.

Abortion ~ think about it

Abortion is one of the most important moral issues facing Irish people today. It has been said that the road to hell is paved with good intentions. I believe that many well-intentioned people have a misguided sense of mercy in relation to the issue of abortion as a choice a woman should be allowed to make for herself.

A woman has the right to control her own body. But the situation gets more complicated when her body has two heartbeats, two different sets of brain waves and two different blood types.

In Ireland, some people seem to be ashamed of our restrictive abortion laws (abortion is permitted to save the life of the mother) when we should actually be proud of them. It is a contentious issue because people feel strongly about it on both sides. There is also a lot of misinformation floating around on social media.

We live in a world where tolerance is revered as a virtue. But one can be tolerant of things that are harmful and abortion is certainly harmful, not only very obviously, to the unborn child but also to society itself.

We live in a permissive age and a time when people want to cast off the shackles of religion and live without moral restraint.

The saturation media coverage has begun in a pro-abortion campaign that is well-funded by foreign money. The press is predominantly pro-abortion, and the issue is making headline news with regular opinion and analysis articles featuring in newspapers.

There will be a lot of sensational reporting which is emotionally manipulative. Data that is incomplete or exaggerated will be misused to promote this secular-humanist agenda.

This push for abortion is not really a grassroots movement. There has been no groundswell of opinion clamouring for this. Rather it is driven by activists and lobbyists have their strategic networks. These are well organised and very effective. I don't doubt the sincerity of some people on the pro-choice side, but I do believe that this agenda is driven by agencies like Amnesty International, Ireland, and many others.

It is inevitable that this issue will provoke debate and division, but we must not be afraid to speak out and to do so with clarity by asserting the right to life of the unborn.

ABORTION DOES NOT MAKE YOU UN-PREGNANT IT MAKES YOU THE MOTHER OF A DEAD BABY!

Some "pro-choice" people might think of access to abortion as an act of mercy. But this is misguided. In order to do that, they have to believe the unborn child is not a living person or be indifferent to that assertion.

Many babies are being aborted in the UK and other countries with "abnormalities" that are certainly not "fatal" such as cleft palate, Down's syndrome (DS), etc. Abortion is permitted up to the time of birth in the UK if there is a DS diagnosis. In any case, what is "normal"?

So 5 minutes before the child is born it has no human rights but five minutes after it is born it mysteriously acquires full human rights ~ unless it is born with a defect in Holland, where it can be killed under the Groningen Protocol or in Sweden, where the gender of the child is sufficient reason to kill it. What kind of society do we want? What are we becoming?

The argument that a woman has the right to control her own body may be correct, but it is not the issue at this point. Because, once she is pregnant, that foetus is entirely separate, distinct, and unique. It is not part of her body, but only dependent on her body for nutrition and a safe environment.

Every human life is of infinite value, and this value is not diminished by the circumstances of that life's beginning. This regard for life is the cornerstone of Western culture. Society is best served by medical ethics that holds this principle sacred.

Scientists claim they are creating human life in a test tube. It can't be called something else in the womb. You can't have it both ways. We have no right to destroy life.

We need to be aware that the permissive agenda will not be satisfied with limited abortion or strict criteria etc. We should be clear that any liberalization of the abortion law is but the first step for those most vigorously proposing abortion. It begins with "updating archaic abortion laws" or "abortion reform" followed by liberal abortion, abortion on demand at any stage (up to birth).

The traditional Western ethic is rooted in the Judeo/Christian tradition. It has always placed great emphasis on the intrinsic worth and equal value of every human life and has been the cornerstone of Western medicine. If this is eroded the collapse of the edifice is only a matter of time.

The Christian duty is to oppose laws which permit abortion. The foetus is a living human being and as such has the right to life. This has been the Christian understanding throughout the history of Western civilisation.

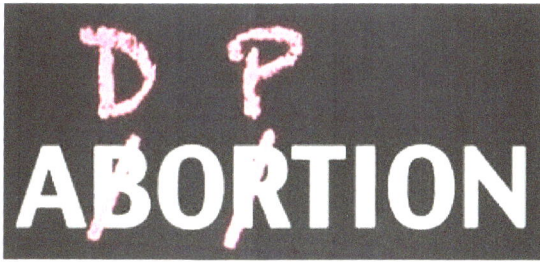

There are very few instances where the baby threatens the life of the mother ~ this is a spurious argument ~ people use this to campaign for permissive abortion on demand, for no medical reason whatsoever. It is the thin end of the wedge. The current situation in Ireland is that the life of the mother is protected if the child is an *actual* threat to her life. Medical authorities in the fields of obstetrics and gynaecology worldwide have stated that in the present day of excellent medical, surgical care the situation rarely exists where the baby must be sacrificed to preserve the life of the mother.

Abortions ostensibly performed for medical reasons are usually justified on psychiatric grounds ~ this is a smoke-screen. There is no established cause and effect connection between pregnancy and mental illness. Women who have psychological problems become pregnant but pregnancy is not the cause of their illness, and abortion is not the cure. The whole notion that a pregnancy might threaten the mental health of the mother is vague and open to abuse and is not sufficient reason to warrant the destruction of her baby.

We might be told that unless an abortion is performed the patient will commit suicide. This claim is fallacious and does not stand up to clinical and statistical scrutiny. It is often an argument used by unscrupulous people who want to get rid of the baby for other reasons.

I wonder how many women have committed suicide because they could not avail of abortion ~ I could not find any statistics to support this argument. On the contrary, it seems that pregnancy has a beneficial effect on the mental well-being of mothers. The reality is that abortion is more detrimental to their health than giving birth because the psychic trauma of abortion persists throughout life. It is curious that feminist groups are not taking account of this.

I don't doubt that an unwanted pregnancy can be a traumatic experience. But with the right support anxieties can be alleviated. Abortion causes more distress than it cures.

Many people eradicate the unborn child for personal convenience ~ a pregnancy is not always convenient. An infant in utero is a person under the law and will continue to be that no matter what the law says. We should not confuse law and morality, and we should not vote in a referendum in a way that would effectively bring about a change in the status of the unborn child. The right thing to do is to vote against any change in the Constitution.

Allowing for abortion is passing death sentences on thousands of unborn children and denying them any right of appeal. A woman should not act as judge, jury, and executioner in the case of an innocent child.

There are those who contend that the mother alone should decide how many children she will have ~ but there are women who are grossly irresponsible who have had multiple abortions. We must not confuse birth control and abortion. If a man and woman engage in sexual intercourse where there is a possibility that pregnancy will occur then they must accept responsibility for the child that has been conceived ~ to kill that child is not just irresponsible it is wrong!

It is the moral duty of all people to protect those who cannot protect themselves. We should support Christian counselling services and other support services for women who have been sexually abused or raped. We should promote the idea of adoption as a positive alternative to abortion. If a mother can be helped to see the value of placing her unwanted child in a childless home, that is a good thing.

The right to life should not be subject to a majority vote. Therefore, we must be resolute in our opposition to abortion. The notion of abortion ought to be repugnant to all who profess faith in Christ because the unborn child is innocent and defenceless and killing is forbidden in Scripture. God has spoken, "You shall not murder" (Exodus 20:13). Since when does a "woman's right to choose" trump God's clearly stated prohibition of murder?

It has often been stated that by not allowing abortions in our hospitals, we compel women to avail of illegal, back-street abortions conducted by unqualified people. So, it is argued that it would be better to permit abortions by competent professionals in order to protect women. But Irish women can and do avail of abortion in the UK and whereas that might be inconvenient for them and add to the expense of the procedure it does negate the "necessity" for back-street abortion. Legalising abortion will decriminalise it but will never make it morally right. Again we need to remember that just because something is legal, it is not necessarily right or good.

We should note too that abortion is a lucrative business and if it is legalised in Ireland, clinics and agencies facilitating this will spring up rapidly. Whatever happened to the Hippocratic Oath ~ "I will give no deadly medicine to anyone if asked, nor suggest any such counsel, and in like manner I will not give to a woman a pessary to procure an abortion." This has been diluted over many years to accommodate what was once deemed abhorrent. It is frightening to think that a doctor will kill a baby in the womb, not out of some misguided sense of altruism but for a fee. To deal with human life as if it is of no value is not right in the eyes of God.

We live in a cruel, inhuman atheistic world where the abortion campaign is driven by secular humanists in a wider agenda. When paediatricians favour abortion, there is something seriously wrong with society. The Christian voice is needed now more than ever to uphold the intrinsic worth and equal value of every human life. The traditional ethic that informs and guides medicine is rooted in the Judeo/Christian culture, which is now being eroded. People are trying to rationalise abortion in a moral vacuum.

The Neoliberal Bandwagon is in Town

"If the cripples are going to die, let them do so, to decrease the surplus population." These are the words of Scrooge discussing Tiny Tim's frail health in A Christmas Carol by Charles Dickens.

The mean-spirited curmudgeon of the much loved Dickens tale is forced to consider his own mortality and consequently repent of his miserly attitudes. His transformation and the positive impact it has on others is a heart-warming story. I only wish that those who advocate the abortion of children who are "crippled" might also consider their status in the light of eternity and undergo a similar conversion.

Dietrich Bonhoeffer (1906-1945) pastor and anti-Nazi dissident executed by hanging in Flossenbürg concentration camp, Germany, condemned abortion:

> Destruction of the embryo in the mother's womb is a violation of the right to live which God has bestowed upon this nascent life. To raise the question whether we are here concerned already with a human being or not is merely to confuse the issue. The simple fact is that God certainly intended to create a human being and that this nascent human being has been deliberately deprived of his life. And that is nothing but murder.

Many people of that generation might have expressed this sentiment in similar words. However, what makes the argument of Bonhoeffer interesting is the fact that he was killed by people who subscribed to a philosophy of life that espoused and enacted the systematic extermination of the handicapped.

The Nazi policy of eugenics proposed the improvement of the human species by encouraging or permitting reproduction of only those people with genetic characteristics judged desirable. The German state under Nazi rule exercised involuntary euthanasia for the mentally and physically disabled. To all right-thinking people this warped ideology was abhorrent. But today in much of Western society unborn children with even minor foetal "abnormalities" are being aborted, infanticide is regularly practiced (babies that survive abortion are killed) and euthanasia is legal in several countries and is becoming more and more acceptable in contemporary culture.

There can be no doubt that abortion is leading to euthanasia. We are now euthanizing people for the same reasons we have been killing unborn people for many decades. The same utilitarian worldview dominates these inextricably linked agendas. The tactics used by both the pro-abortion and pro-euthanasia movements are the same. And the same personnel are clamouring for both.

It will be interesting to hear the pro-abortionists in Ireland try to deny that the unborn child is a human being. They have done this and will continue to do this as they deceptively lead people like the Pied Piper of Hamelin into captivity. However, elsewhere in the world pro-abortionists have moved on from such denials. They have had to do this because the scientific facts have wrong-footed them on this issue. So, in order not to be knocked off balance they have acknowledged that pre-born babies are human beings. But they contend that their killing (and it is never called murder/homicide, as that is a legal term for "unlawful" killing) is sanctioned and protected by the state where they live.

Therefore, pro-abortionists in other countries (like the USA) have abandoned, for the most part, the argument that the unborn are not human beings. They now simply shrug their shoulders and say, "So what? Abortion is legal." This repulsive attitude is disturbingly common among more and more people as society becomes progressively desensitized to this sort of killing.

This emerging genocidal mindset among pro-abortionists is where Ireland is headed. We might deny it now, but in time this will be the overt attitude of pro-abortionists in this country too. It needs to be said, over and over again, without fear that abortion is murder. What else would one call the deliberate ending of a life? No doctor involved in the procedure is under any illusion to the contrary. They may justify it in their own terms and engage in semantics and employ euphemistic terms as a smokescreen for the reality of what they are doing. But they know they are stopping a beating heart and thus terminating a life.

I am saddened to see celebrities like Liam Neeson acting as a cheerleader for the Pied Piper of Hamelin as he plays his hypnotic tune. The people of this nation are being led on a merry dance to a dungeon of darkness.

To all those jumping on the neoliberal bandwagon, my views are irrelevant. The pro-abortion agenda is contextualised as "progressive" and to oppose it is seen as anti-women. I have already been accused of "scaremongering." The perception is that people who resist and oppose the abortion campaign are Neanderthals. For me to say that "abortion is neither contraception nor medical care" is seen misogynistic. To uphold the sanctity of the life of the unborn is to be labelled a Bible-thumping, heartless freak who is out of touch with reality. Name-calling and negative labelling are to be expected now in a culture where tolerance is revered as a virtue, and political correctness gags any dissenting voice to the prevailing orthodoxy.

I want to remind the pro-choice movement that there are limits to choice and consequences too. Rights come with responsibilities. But I suspect that will be heard as strident preaching.

Norman Mailer[19] has said, "I am perfectly willing to grant that life starts at conception. If a woman doesn't want to have a child, then I think it's her right to say no. But let's not pretend that it isn't a form of killing." At least he was honest and didn't pretend he was supporting abortion as a benign and innocuous procedure. So, I'm calling on the pro-choice lobby to admit that they want the killing of human beings and, to be honest and acknowledge that they don't care about that so long as it is legalised.

The pro-choice movement has a secular-humanist agenda that is inherently anti-religious. It sets itself against the canons, conventions, and customs of the past in a reactionary way, rejecting what it perceives as antiquated and oppressive. But we are being exhorted to throw the baby out with the bathwater. They are beguiling the Irish people into thinking that they are heralding a better society when they are actually ushering in a culture of death.

---

[19] Norman Mailer (1923-2007) was an American novelist, journalist, essayist, playwright, film-maker, actor, and political activist.

The Bridge between Abortion and Euthanasia Is Infanticide

The bridge between abortion and euthanasia is infanticide. This practice is well embedded in the medical profession of countries where abortion is legally permitted. In other words, it is now "normal." But not very long ago it caused enough concern to see these kinds of cases brought to court. Things have moved on significantly since then. Many abortionists no longer deny that the unborn child is a human being; they shrug and say, "So what? It's legal." We now have abortion permitted up to the time of birth ~ for example in the U.K. where a diagnosis of Down's syndrome is given or in the Netherlands infanticide practiced legally under a medical code known as the Groningen Protocol. "Pro-choice" campaigners in Ireland are openly calling for abortion without limits and for any reason whatsoever.

However, it might be of interest to note some of the early cases that have ultimately led to a public desensitisation on this issue. This historical connection between abortion and infanticide is evident in the following three cases in the USA.[20]

1. The Edelin Case.

On October 3, 1973, Kenneth Edelin from Boston performed an abortion on a 17-year old girl who was 24 weeks pregnant. His saline abortion attempt failed, so he performed a caesarean abortion the next day. He detached the placenta (cutting off blood oxygenation to the baby) and held the child inside the mother's uterus for three minutes as he watched the clock. Satisfied that the baby was finally dead, he removed it and disposed of it. A pathologist testified that the

---

[20] I have related these three case histories almost verbatim as they are recorded in the *Pro-Life Activist's Encyclopedia* published by American Life League.

baby had been able to take at least one breath before Edelin suffocated it. Edelin was charged and convicted of manslaughter by a jury, but the verdict was thrown out by an appeals court on a minor technicality. It is significant that the court system overrode the verdict of a jury in favour of expanding abortion "rights" to include infanticide.

2. The Waddill Case.

Benjamin Waddill, an abortionist, and member of the Association of Planned Parenthood Physicians, performed a saline abortion on 19-year old Mary Weaver on March 2, 1977, at California's Westminster Community Hospital. Mary Weaver knew that she was at least 28 weeks pregnant, well into the third trimester. Her baby was healthy, she was not a victim of rape or incest or health problems, but she still wanted an abortion so she would not embarrass her father, who was principal of the high school that she had attended. This is an example of third-trimester abortion for social reasons ~ a phenomenon that some pro-abortionists deny. After doing the saline infusion, Waddill left the scene. Later, he phoned the hospital and talked to a nurse who informed him that a viable baby had resulted from his abortion. Waddill instructed her, "Don't do a goddamn thing for that baby." He then returned to the hospital's newborn nursery, where the baby had been relocated, and ordered the area cleared of all medical personnel. He then choked Baby Girl Weaver four separate times, by pushing down on her windpipe with his thumb.

Dr. Ronald Cornelson, the attending paediatrician, witnessed the entire sequence of events and subsequently brought charges against Waddill. During the trial, the prosecutor presented a taped phone conversation in which Waddill told Cornelson to, "not get squirrely and stick to the story as we discussed." He maintained that he had merely put his hand on her throat to check her pulse.

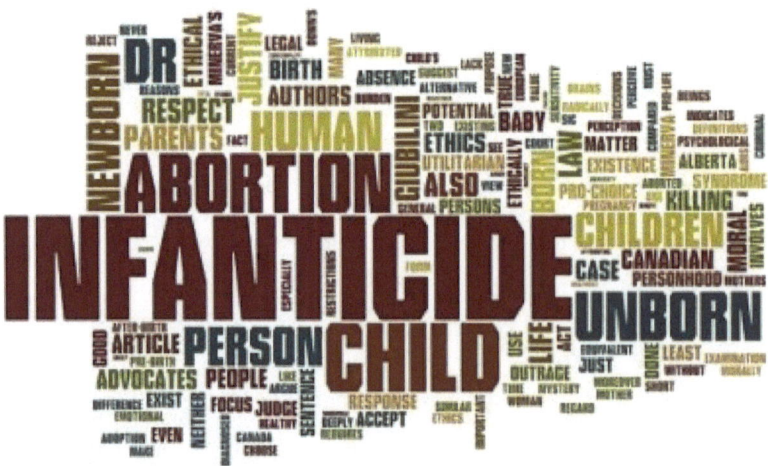

However, the prosecutor also showed that Waddill had explained to several people that he choked the baby girl to death because he feared that lawsuits would be filed against him if the baby survived.

The mother of the baby sued Waddill, claiming that she would never have gone through with the abortion if he had informed her that she might give birth to a live baby. Sadly, botched abortions like this will only serve to make the killers more effective and efficient so there will be less evidence of the reality that the baby is a human being.

At Waddill's trial, Judge James K. Turner instructed the jury to ignore the classical definition of death — cessation of all vital signs. It took the jury a week to come to a decision with 7 of the 12 jurors voting for acquittal.

3. The Laufe Case

Dr Leonard Laufe of West Penn Hospital in Pittsburgh, Pennsylvania, specialised in late-term abortions. In 1985, a woman falsely claimed that she had been raped and Laufe aborted her 32-week baby. The prostaglandin abortion (which induces uterine contractions) resulted in the baby being born alive. The baby began to gasp and kick, and Nurse Monica Bright testified that Laufe ordered that no help be given to the child. In fact, one of the staff doctors ordered nurses to kill the child with a fatal injection of morphine directly. At least three nurses refused to kill the child. The entire episode, including close-ups of the baby gasping and kicking, was filmed for "educational purposes."

The original birth records indicated that the little girl weighed more than three pounds and was 18 inches long. In order to cover up his killing, Dr. Laufe altered hospital records to read a weight of two and a half pounds and a length of only 11 inches.

Medical student John Kenny testified that Dr. Laufe's attorney threatened that, if he testified in court, he would never be able to get a medical license or practice in any hospital in Pennsylvania.

Dr. Laufe claimed that the baby was dead at birth. Despite the film of the entire episode, he was acquitted of all charges.

Times have Changed

Times have changed and not for the better. Today when a viable human life is extracted from the womb it is killed by lethal injection, or put in a refrigerator, or left to die as a matter of routine. We now have in some constituencies partial birth abortions where a perfectly healthy baby is killed as it is being born and for no other reason than it is unwanted.

People tend to confuse law with morality, and the legal outcomes of the three cases mentioned above have contributed significantly to a shift in attitudes that have become more accepting of this reality.

First, it is acceptable to kill an unborn child; then it is acceptable to kill a viable baby that survives abortion, then it becomes acceptable to kill a neo-natal infant, then it becomes acceptable to kill a toddler, a teenager, an adult. There will be (and there are) many reasons given to "justify" this, but the reality is that we are now entering a culture of death where the vulnerable and the aged are exposed to the very real threat that they may be exterminated for someone's convenience. Abortion and euthanasia are part of the same secular-humanist agenda.

Just as you cannot have a culture of female infanticide without other catastrophic consequences in society ~ as in India where respect for women is extremely low and rape is common ~ so too you cannot have a culture that approves the killing of children without that in turn unravelling the fabric of society.

The vital role of physicians as healers in society must be preserved, and the important but neglected spiritual dimension of death must be explored. Thus, a biblical view of human life needs to be presented in society.

Death and bereavement are universal phenomena, and people of all faiths and those of none have a legitimate right to comment. However, the historic Christian tradition is struggling to be heard in the clamour for personal autonomy and civil liberties in a multi-cultural society that is becoming increasingly secular. We need an ethical framework in which euthanasia and assisted suicide can be evaluated. These issues are on the radar indicating a collision course with Christian values. It is time for Christians to be alert and to present the case that these are not satisfactory solutions to legitimate end-of-life concerns.